Internet Success For Beginners

7 Secrets Revealed

INTERNET SUCCESS FOR BEGINNERS

7 Secrets Revealed

Madeleine Kay

Chrysalis Publishing

DEDICATION

To all my fellow techno-phobes
and techno-dummies . . .

There *is* hope!

BOOKS IN THE INTERNET SUCCESS SERIES

Whether you are a beginner on the computer, a techno-phobe, a novice computer or business person, a budding entrepreneur . . . or just someone who wants to create a successful business on the internet without "reinventing the wheel" or wading through the avalanche of information to learn how to do what you want, my new series of internet marketing books on the subject of internet success will help you discover how to create a successful internet business simply, easily, quickly and inexpensively.

This series includes the following books and will be available in both paperback and digital formats. Some books in the series may not yet be available, but will be shortly, so check back for these . . . and for other books that may be added to the series.

Internet Success for Beginners . . . 7 Secrets Revealed
(A guide for the true beginner)

*Internet Success for Beginning Entrepreneurs
. . . 7 Secrets Revealed*
(A guide for the novice entrepreneur)

Internet Success . . . 12 Secrets Revealed
(Combines both of the above *Internet Success*
books in one volume)

*Millionaire Marketing . . . How to Make
the Internet Work for You*
(A guide to some broad marketing concepts
for the internet)

ACKNOWLEDGMENTS

To my good friend and graphic designer
– Claire Collins –
without whom none of this would be possible.
Thank you so much!

And many thanks to Zaldy Icaonapo
for the sensational cover image.

BOOKS BY MADELEINE KAY

The Serendipity Handbook

Scats . . . scattered thoughts on just about everything

For information on *all* products and services –
books, e-books, e-courses, coaching, consulting,
"fun stuff". . . and more
visit www.madeleinekay.com

CONTENTS

A NOTE FROM THE AUTHOR

This is the first in a series of books on creating a successful internet business . . . and doing it simply, easily, quickly and inexpensively.

Each of the books can be read by itself, without reading any of the others. Or, if you read all of them, you can read them in any order you choose, since each book is complete in itself. (Some of the books may not yet be completed or available at the time of this writing, so check back for new additions to the series.)

All the books are written very simply and clearly, with information that is non-technical and simple enough for anyone to understand and be able to use.

It is my hope that by making the subject simple, clear and uncomplicated, you will realize that you actually *can* do this . . . and will.

EnjOy,

Madeleine

INTRODUCTION

After publishing my first book and working relentlessly for three years to get into all the traditional major distribution systems and venues, I realized that is not the way to go. Online was the way – a way I knew nothing about . . . and cared even less about, since I was a major techno-phobe.

Nevertheless, I forced myself to forge through the online world and spent the next three to four years doing what I liked least and learning about what I didn't even care for – the internet, computer sales and marketing . . . and that whole cyber-world.

By the time I learned what I needed to know and actually began to understand it so my head stopped spinning and I stopped getting dizzy every time I sat in front of a computer . . . everything had changed and the internet world had advanced and exploded.

Nevertheless, those three to four years of study helped me quickly learn and assimilate the new information and put it to practical use. (Probably because I used to have my own advertising, marketing and PR agency, so I managed to develop a huge amount of "stickiness" regarding the important things – the simple things – the fast and easy things about online marketing and making money in the internet world.)

Now, I want to share with you what I have learned – so you don't have to spend the agonizingly laborious three to four years that I did learning all this and assimilating it, so it actually becomes usable information, rather than just disorganized clutter in your brain.

I'm not going to talk about the most obvious or the very complicated, technical or expensive ways to succeed on the internet. There are plenty of books out there on those . . . and I imagine that most of you are not looking for complicated, expensive or technical. My guess is that most of you want simple, easy, fast and inexpensive . . . or even, free.

So, here goes – as simply and succinctly as possible – to help you get started creating your own internet business success. Here are 7 really simple, easy-to-do, inexpensive secrets I have learned about creating success online.

(Resources and links to what I have found to be the best, most helpful and inexpensive companies to help you, are listed throughout the book . . . and also, at the back of the book – *with phone numbers whenever possible*, for those of you who, like me, prefer to speak to a live person rather than getting your information from and asking your questions via e-mail. Most, but not all of these, are companies that I use, and have used for years.)

Secret #1

CREATE AN AFFILIATE SITE
OR SITES

This can be done for practically no money at all . . . or even, completely free! (More about that later.)

You can do it for a $9.49-$11.99 annual domain fee, plus $48 - $60 a year hosting fee for basic hosting . . . and that's it!

You can get your domain name and hosting at Go Daddy (www.godaddy.com) . . . and get your affiliates and get paid through ClickBank (www.clickbank.com), which has no up-front costs or fees . . . they only take a very small percentage once something has sold.

Let me explain the fees – which are ridiculously minimal – and explain what an affiliate site is.

As I said, ClickBank is completely free to sign up with and has no up-front costs. They make their money by taking a very small percentage (approximately 7.5% plus a $1.00 transaction fee) from what you get paid AFTER someone purchases something through your affiliate link.

What is an affiliate site? It's a site on which you list (and promote, if you wish) other people's products and services. All the products and services on ClickBank are digital, probably because those are the simplest, fastest, easiest and usually, the highest profit items to list, promote and deliver.

So you don't have to actually sell anything. You don't carry any inventory. You don't have to write, produce, create or distribute anything. You don't even have to write any sales copy. It's all done for you automatically. You are just the "middle man" (or "middle person") letting people know about it.

How do you let them know? By putting up a web page. I recommend putting it up on Go Daddy (www.godaddy.com). There are others, but I have used Go Daddy for ten years and have found them to be excellent. (Another one growing in popularity, that you might want to check out, is www.intuit.com, which is also simple and inexpensive.)

Go Daddy is an internet company for anyone and everyone – they truly offer internet services "for dummies," and techno-phobes. Their service is great! It's fast, simple and really inexpensive. Their service people are really knowledgeable and helpful – and are always available – 24/7!

So, you can buy any domain name that is available, through Go Daddy . . . and even sign up for names that are not currently available, but will or may be coming available.

Once you get your domain name, you can use their simple templates to put up your site.

Once your site is up – you get affiliate links or banner ads (whichever you prefer) to put up on your site. Then, every time someone clicks on your link or banner and purchases one of those products or services, you receive a commission . . . often as high as 75% - 80% of the sale price.

Again, you do not have to deliver the product or service . . . or create it. You are merely providing a link, directing people to the website at which they can learn about it and purchase it if they wish to. If they do purchase, then you receive a commission just for connecting them.

How and where do you get affiliate links to or banner ads for these products and services? An easy way is to go to ClickBank (www.clickbank.com) and sign up as an affiliate. It's free!

Then go to their marketplace and just click on the categories and products and services you want to promote . . . and ClickBank will create what they call a hop ad for you to put on your website or web page

. . . and that's it!

You can even do this without having a website or page! Remember I said you can create an affiliate business absolutely free? Well, if you don't want to buy a domain name . . . if you don't want to put up a web site or web page . . . you can still do this. How?

After you select the products or services you want to promote, ClickBank will create two things for you – one is the hop ad for your website or page (it is in html format) and the other is a hoplink – which is simply a text link that you can send out in e-mails to friends, family, associates, etc. By doing this via e-mail, you are in essence, creating your own affiliate business absolutely free . . . you don't even need a domain name or a website.

ClickBank will automatically calculate your commission and will send you monthly checks (once you submit your payment information to them) – within 60 days of purchase to allow for returns (since their return policy is 60 days).

It's as simple as that – fast, easy, simple, and inexpensive . . . even possible for absolutely free!

There are lots of other sites and places to find affiliates. Two others are PayDotCom (www.paydotcom.com) and Commission Junction (www.cj.com), which give you the opportunity to become an affiliate for physical products as well as digital ones.

I've used ClickBank and I know many people who have also used it. It seems to offer a wide variety of excellent affiliate options and is really simple to use and set up. I have not used PayDotCom, but it has grown very quickly and become very popular . . . and is certainly worth your checking out.

Commission Junction is a very well-respected affiliate program company that has been around for awhile and is quite extensive. It is used by a lot of individuals, as well as large companies, to promote their products and services and is definitely worth checking out. I found it a bit more complicated than ClickBank . . . and have not actually used it myself, although I know of many people who have.

(FYI – I believe Commission Junction requires you to have a minimum monthly dollar amount of transactions and it charges a dormant account fee, if you have not had any transactions for six months. If you do want to use Commission Junction, make sure you read their entire agreement before signing up. You should, of course, *always* read the entire agreement, all the rules, fees, etc. prior to signing anything with any company, individual or business.)

Secret #2

CREATE A DIRECTORY SITE

What is a directory site? It is merely a site that lists information about people or places that offer a particular product or service within a specific industry or subject area. The site directs people to these companies, places, individuals or sites, where they can find and get what they are looking for in a particular industry, region, state, area, subject, etc.

The nature and complexity or simplicity of your site will depend upon how much you know about computers and how much time you want to spend on the computer and setting up your site.

Simply pick an industry, subject, area, region

or state that you want to focus on . . . and then find and list companies, services, products or individuals in that arena on your site.

There are many different ways you can do this and approaches you can take.

One way is to do this site similar to an affiliate site. The main difference is that the easiest way to do an affiliate site is for only digital and downloadable products and services. So, you can find the affiliate links all in one or two places, if you want.

(Affiliate sites can also be for physical products, but then you usually have to search the internet to see who has an affiliate program and sign up for each one separately. It's time con-suming and not nearly as effective or productive. Two of the exceptions to this, as I mentioned, are PayDotCom (www.paydotcom.com) and Commission Junction (www.cj.com), which let you sign up to become an affiliate for both physical and digital products – all in one place.)

With a directory site, you have more freedom to create one broad general site – and then create lots of sub sites for that . . . i.e. computers, then break that category down into regions, cities, products, etc. So each directory site you have can generate many mini sites that are more targeted ones. In this way, you can blanket a market and blitz the internet.

You can list the same places on several of your sites and then link them – the search engines love links. The more you are linked, the more the search engines pick you up . . . and the links connect people who go to one of your sites, to all your others.

You can even create a national directory site for different subjects, industries, etc. by zip code. Go to www.pizza.com to see what I am talking about (as of the date of this writing), but I imagine that would take a bit of tech savvy to set up.

So, how do you make money from a directory site? Several ways . . .

One way to make money is by listing companies, individuals and sites with affiliate links, so you receive a commission when a sale is made through your link.

A second way is to charge a listing fee, and I would recommend making it so affordable, that they feel they cannot pass it up . . . they feel – why not list on your site. Rather than making a large profit on individual sales and listings, make your profit in quantity of sales. Make people an offer they can't refuse! Charge your "listers" a monthly fee or a reduced annual fee, if they pay for the year in advance. Then give them a ridiculously discounted rate if they list on multiple sites of yours.

A third way to make money from directory sites is to sell advertising on your site. Again – make people an offer they can't refuse – offer them a ridiculous rate, and again, offer them annual and multiple site discounts.

The fourth way to make money from a directory site is to have a monthly newsletter, which helps you create a data base. And . . . you don't even have to write the newsletter. Offer the opportunity to a different advertiser or "lister" each month. (You can also sell advertising in the newsletter . . . and/or sponsorships.) This creates loyalty and continuity from and for your advertisers, listers and mailing list members.

All of these things (listings, advertising, sponsorships, mailing list for newsletter) help you create a data base that adds real value to your business and your site. So, after you've built it up over a few years, you put the site up for sale and auction it off through companies like Sedo (www.sedo.com) or Go Daddy's Domain Name After Market (TDNAM at www.godaddy.com).

If you have a good domain name . . . plus income coming in from advertisers and listers . . . plus a database, you may be able to sell your site (or business) for a lot of money (just like people sell their businesses offline). The guy who owned pizza. com sold his site and domain name for $1.3 million in 2008 on sedo.com – and it's a relatively easy-to-create site!

Secret #3

SELL DOMAIN NAMES

This brings me to the third secret to making money on the internet. If you own good domain names . . . or for a relatively small amount, decide to purchase some good ones – then put them up for auction on Go Daddy's Domain Name After Market (TDNAM) site at www.godaddy.com or on Sedo (www.sedo.com) and sell the names.

You can put up a parked page that announces that the name is for sale . . . or you can even put up an actively functioning site and sell the name. Even if you have a website already up, you can auction off the name.

In addition to GoDaddy and Sedo, there are other domain name management companies that do auctions – both online and offline. At the time of this writing, a company called Oversee (www. oversee.net) and Snap Names (www.snapnames.com a division of oversee.net) held a live auction in Fort Lauderdale, Florida which netted a total of $2,386,550 for 35 domain names. One of them, www.dating.com sold for $1.75 million – the highest bid among the 120 names up for sale at the DomainFest live auction. All the names that were not sold at the live auction, were added to an extended online auction.

Just think of websites as online real estate. That's what they actually are. Websites and domains are the new real estate . . . and online and the internet are the new property locations.

Be careful to read all the rules, regulations and small print when selling or auctioning off your site or domain name. There are several different kinds of auctions – you can declare a reserve amount below which you won't go (and if someone offers an amount equal to your reserve, I believe you must sell it then). You can put it up under "make an offer." There are 7-day auctions and 30 and 90 day auctions. There are premium listings you can pay for so your listing gets noticed more.

So, if you do decide to sell or auction your sites or domain names, make sure you have read and understood all the terms, responsibilities, caveats, binders, and whatever else there is in the small print. It can get very complicated, very competitive, very exciting . . . and of course, there are a lot of legalities involved. So read everything thoroughly, carefully . . . and always consult with your business, investment, financial, legal advisor before doing or signing anything.

Secret #4

CAPITALIZE ON PUBLIC DOMAIN PRODUCTS

Use public domain material for your site. What does public domain mean? It means that no one holds the copyright on it.

There are many public domain books out there that you can download from a variety of public domain sites like www.gutenburg.org . . . and then sell them on your site for $.99 each. Believe me the $.99 adds up – look at iTunes and the Dollar Stores!

You can do this with books . . . and also with photographs. There are a lot of magnificent government photos on space, nature, etc. However, it's a lot more work to upload photo images and create a site with high-quality downloadable images, than it is with books and text products.

The service you are providing that makes it worth the $.99 to people – is convenience. They don't have to go to all different public domain sites to find what they are looking for . . . you've already done that for them. Of course, you don't call your site a public domain site . . . and it is your choice whether to mention that what you are offering is in the public domain. I suggest being up front about it and letting people know exactly what they are getting and that you are merely charging for the convenience of having done all the legwork for them and of having it all in one place for them.

Be sure to check the copyright information on all public domain books. Anything published prior to 1929 is in the public domain. But after 1929, it gets tricky because there are different copyright coverage periods and rules after that, so go to www.copyright.gov to check it out completely.

Also, if you are offering translations of foreign works (the original work published prior to 1929, but the translation after), make sure to check out whether that translation is, in fact, in the public domain.

Another service you are offering by doing this is bringing a lot of these older great and/or little known books to the public awareness and helping to make them popular and accessible again.

A Note . . . Just Google "public domain books". . . and a lot of sites will come up, from which you can learn about and get information on public domain books and download them. Always be sure to check the freedom of usage information on each site for the public domain books you download . . . and/or any public domain products you wish to sell or offer, to make sure they can be resold commercially.

Secret #5

SET UP A STORE AT CAFE PRESS

If you are an artist – or a writer – and have either great ideas and/or images that you want to put on different products, but you don't want to carry inventory, or be responsible for producing and manufacturing the products, or be responsible for delivery or order taking or fulfillment – Café Press is ideal for you. (www.cafepress.com)

It is a very popular, international site that allows you to place your unique and individual sayings, ideas, logo and art work on hundreds of products to sell. It doesn't cost you anything to do this . . . the cost of producing each item is deducted from the sale price, *after* someone orders and purchases it. So there is no out-of-pocket cost to you to create, produce or sell these items.

Café Press has two kinds of stores that you can set up – Basic and Premium. The Basic store is completely free to set up and a great way to start to build up inventory and customers. Of course, it is more limited than the Premium Store, in terms of what you can offer and how you can set up and customize your store.

The Basic Store allows you to offer only one of each item . . . and you cannot customize the appearance of your store. But as I said – it's free – and a great way to start, until you have both a customer and a product base.

The Premium store costs $6.95 per month (or $18.45 if you pay for 3 months in advance, $34.95 if pay for 6 months, and $59.95 if you pay for a year) – and it lets you completely customize the appearance of your store . . . and you can offer as many different variations on, or sayings and images on or for, each item.

Their retail base price is very high however, so your mark up on each item will probably not be that great. But, since each item is custom-printed, people are willing to pay the higher prices if they like your saying or image . . . and . . . you will make your money, hopefully, in volume, rather than having a big profit margin on each item.

Also – it's a great way to get your name, product, service, ideas, images and your "branding" out there. Think of it as free advertising. Not only is it free . . . you get paid for putting your "brand" out there and on those products for people to buy, use, wear and enjoy.

And . . . Café Press even has an affiliate program. So, you can be an affiliate and promote other people's products . . . and they can be affiliates and promote yours.

(Another site growing in popularity that allows artists and crafts people to sell their products is www.etsy.com. You sign up for free and can customize your shop. Then it costs only $.20 per item to list it for four months. When it sells, you pay a 3.5% transaction fee. Something you might want to check out.)

Secret #6

CREATE SUB-CATEGORIES AND SUB-SITES

For just about all of these secrets – once you've created one or two main sites – you can easily create a plethora of sub sites. I touched on the subject a bit while explaining Secret #2 – Creating a Directory Site.

You can do this with directory sites, affiliate sites, public domain products sites . . . even your Café Press stores

You can literally break any broad, general category site into specific smaller sub sites – using the same templates – and often, a lot of the same listings.

For example – the broad category of com-

45

puters can be broken down into ink cartridges and toners, printers, screens, service, retailers, etc . . . and then these can be broken down into regions, states, cities, etc.

So one site can generate many – each linked, sometimes with some overlaps, all of which help you establish a real presence on the internet and the search engines and kind of blitz the internet and dominate a category, to a certain degree.

Or you can really diversify and have just one site in each of a multitude of different categories to cover and hit all different segments of the internet market.

Again, it's your choice how you want to go – wide and broad, or in-depth and specific.

Secret #7

LINK ALL YOUR SITES

To exponentially multiply the reach and scope of your sites, you can link all of them.

The search engines love links . . . and the more your sites are linked, the more the search engines pick them up more easily. And . . . the more easily people on the internet find and get to all your different sites.

And the linking is not just limited to within each type of site. If you decide to do affiliate sites, directory sites, public domain sites, Café Press stores, or develop sub-sites of any or all of these, you can link all of them – and in that way, really cross section

47

the internet market and optimize your exposure and sales possibilities.

Linking is very easy to do. You can put up a Links and Resources page (or if you prefer, call it a Recommendations page) on your website(s), and on that page, just list the different website names, providing a link for people to click on and be taken to that site.

Or you can write a short blurb describing each of the different sites you are linking to (in addition to providing a link to get to it) . . . or, if you prefer, you can even create an image (or take images from the various sites) and post them on your Links and Resources (or your Recommendations) page . . . with a short blurb next to each image, describing the site and letting people know what it offers when they click on the link you provide. Since this is all done on the internet, always make sure you provide a live link for people to click on to be taken to the other site(s).

FYI . . .

You'll be happy to know that you can implement most of these 7 secrets – your affiliate sites, directory sites, public domain sites, Café Press stores, and sub-categories – without having to pay for separate hosting for each one or without having to purchase a lot of different domain names.

Again, I am going to use Go Daddy (www. godaddy.com) as the model because it is truly the only company that I – as a recovering techno-phobe and techno-dummy – use and am absolutely thrilled, delighted and satisfied with. They are so helpful, reliable, always available, make their products and services easy to use and set up, and are ridiculously inexpensive.

So – if you don't want to purchase a lot of different domain names, but do want to set up a lot of different sites, you can get their economy hosting for $4.99 a month (or $47.88 a year), less any coupon or "Deal of the Day" discounts they are offering. Use one main domain name like uronline.com and then just add each separate page or category as an indexed page (ie: www.uronline.com/computers). As you create subcategories under that, just add another forward slash (/) . . . or for different categories, replace the word "computers" with the new category word.

Or, if you already have a lot of domain names – or want to purchase several and use them – you can purchase Go Daddy's deluxe hosting for $7.99 a month (or $83.88 a year). Remember to ask for the "Deal of the Day" or any coupons or discounts they are offering, which are usually from 15% to 25%. (The advantage of the deluxe hosting is that it has 150 gigs, while the basic has only 10 gigs . . . so you can host multiple domains for the one hosting fee.)

To host multiple domains, you just put each separate domain name up as a separate folder under that one main hosting account. Go Daddy will guide you to, through, and with the instructions on how to do this, if you have any difficulty. (You can also index pages with the deluxe hosting, just as you can with the economy hosting).

So, whichever way you choose to go, you are only paying for hosting once, even though you are putting up a lot of different pages, websites, or domains.

The main thing is to keep it as simple and inexpensive as possible, at least at the beginning, until you develop more computer savvy, a larger customer base, and a momentum. Each of these secrets is simple, easy and expandable. They can be kept as simple as you choose . . . or be developed, elaborated and expanded as much as you want. The choice is yours.

The easiest, simplest and least costly way to set up a payment system – if you are not getting paid by ClickBank, Commission Junction or PayDotCom, is to set up a Pay Pal account. (www.paypal.com) It's free to set up and they only take a small transaction fee and percentage out of every payment . . . that's all!

AFTERWORD

So . . . obviously there is a lot of crossover between these 7 secrets, but there doesn't have to be. You can choose to implement only one of these secrets, you can choose to keep things as simple as you want, or you can expand them to cover all the suggestions and possible permutations I have suggested.

The point of this whole book is to show you that you *can* do it! It's *easier* than you think! You *can* create a viable internet business quickly with no special technical skills; without any unique product or service of your own that you have created or offer:

without having to carry, deliver, distribute or manage any inventory . . . and without even having to do any bookkeeping. And all this can be done inexpensively – and often, even for free!

So there is no up-front layout of any, or much money for you to get started. All your excuses for not starting . . . for not being able to begin or to do it . . . are eliminated. So – what are you waiting for? Begin! Begin now . . . it's very empowering . . . and could be very lucrative!

EnjOy!

Madeleine

ABOUT THE AUTHOR

Madeleine Kay is the Best Selling Author of *Serendipitously Rich* and *Living Serendipitously.* Adventurist, unconventional success and motivation coach . . . and maverick entrepreneur, she has been featured in *Who's Who of American Women* and *Who's Who in the World.*

Former President and Creative Director of her own advertising and marketing agency, she combines a practical real-life knowledge of business marketing with a hard-earned, nose-to-the-grindstone knowledge of internet marketing . . . to simplify, clarify, consolidate and explain some of the many current simple business opportunities online.

Considered America's leading expert on *serendipity*, she brings the wisdom, passion and playfulness of serendipity sprinkled with her own unique brand of practical, down-to-earth common sense to the world of business to help people get, claim and enjoy the riches they desire.

. . . .

To learn about upcoming events; coaching, consulting
and mentoring assistance; online courses;
and upcoming books, e-books and other "fun stuff"
. . . go to www.madeleinekay.com

OTHER BOOKS BY MADELEINE KAY

Serendipitously Rich . . .
How to Get Delightfully, Delectably, Deliciously Rich
(or anything else you want)
in 7 Ridiculously Easy Steps

Changing *if* I am rich to *when* I am rich has never been simpler . . . or more fun. Refreshingly original and excitingly new, *Serendipitously Rich* shows you how to stop struggling and how to start getting rich (and everything else you want) . . . with effortless ease and unmitigated joy.

Living Serendipitously . . . keeping the wonder alive

A lively and joyful read, *Living Serendipitously* gets you to be an *active dreamer*, who is living your dreams, not just thinking about them. It captures the joyful essence of "the art of living" and shows you how to feel deliciously *alive,* vibrant and happy

57

every day of your life . . . no matter what your circumstances. Einstein said, "There are only two ways to live your life – as though nothing is a miracle or as though everything is a miracle." *Living Serendipitously* aligns us with the *everything*.

Living with Outrageous Joy

Joy is contagious . . . joy is revitalizing . . . joy is what every one of us wants to feel more of in our lives every single day. This charming little gift book will re-ignite that feeling of joy in your life and your passion for living. Playfully inspiring and motivating, *Living with Outrageous Joy* will delight and revitalize you. It will open you up to the joy and adventure of living your life to the fullest every single day . . . unleashing in you that feeling of *aliveness* that so many of us are longing to feel.

The 7 Secrets to Living with Joy and Riches

Joy and riches – we all want lots of both! This delightfully inspiring gift book, with its insightful and pithy sayings, will help you discover how to *savor* your life . . . not just work at it. *The 7 Secrets to Living with Joy and Riches* will reunite the longings of your soul with the desires of your flesh . . . so you get, claim and enjoy all the joy and riches you desire.

The 12 Myths About Money

Money! We all need it . . . Everyone wants it . . . Nobody wants to admit they care about it . . . And we all wish we had more – Lots more! So why isn't everyone rich? *The 12 Myths About Money* reveals your hidden core beliefs that may be keeping you from becoming rich, and shows you how to instantly replace them with new beliefs that will empower you to think and act like "The Rich" do. The simple *action plan* helps you begin making these new beliefs work for you – now . . . so you can get, claim and enjoy all the riches you desire. (Currently available as e-book at www.madeleinekay.com)

The UMM Factor
(what you need in order to succeed)

Madeleine Kay's groundbreaking book about passion, purpose and prosperity reveals the three things everyone must have in order to succeed. Without all three, it is possible to succeed, but not likely. With them – your success is guaranteed. What are these three magical things? She calls them *The UMM Factor*.

LINKS AND RESOURCES

Café Press – www.cafepress.com
Tel. 877-809-1659 (9am – 9pm EST, M-Sat)
Production and Fullfillment Company for Digital
Images on Products

ClickBank – www.clickbank.com
Tel. 208-345-4245 (7am – 6pm MST, M-F)
Affiliate Products and Services (Digital and
Downloadable)

Commission Junction – www.cj.com
Tel. 800-761-1072 (6am – 5pm PST, M-F)
Affiliate Products and Services (Physical and Digital)

Etsy – www.etsy.com – support@etsy.com
Online Buying and Selling Community for Handmade
Items

Go Daddy – www.godaddy.com
Tel. 480-505-8820 (Live person 24/7)
Websites, Hosting, Domain Names, The Domain
Name After Market (TDNAM)

Intuit – www.intuit.com
Tel. 877-683-3280 (6am – 5pm PST, M-F)
Websites, Hosting, QuickBooks, Payment Solutions

PayDotCom – www.paydotcom.com
Tel. 888-368-0266 (10am – 6pm, EST)
Affiliate Products and Services (Physical and Digital)

PayPal – www.paypal.com
Tel. 888-847-2747
Payment Service

Oversee – www.oversee.net
Tel. 213-408-0080 (Corporate office in Los Angeles),
954-861-3500 (Florida office of Moniker, division of
Oversee that organized The DomainFest live auction)
www.snapnames.com
Tel. 503-219-9990 (Oregon office of Snap Names
Division)
Domain Management and Sale Company

Sedo – www.sedo.com
Tel. 617-499-7200 (9am – 6pm EST)
Domain Names for Sale Internationally

. . . .

Madeleine Kay is the Founder of the *Serendipity Day Holiday*, celebrated August 18th. You can learn about this exciting new event and how to live serendipitously all year long at . . .
www.serendipitydayholiday.com

Browse serendipity wearables, carryables, and other "fun stuff" at *The Serendipity Shoppe* at . . .
www.cafepress.com/serendip_shoppe

Receive a FREE copy of *The Serendipity Handbook* at . . . www.facebook.com/serendipityday

Also receive a FREE *7 Myths about money* E-course and E-book at . . . www.madeleinekay.com

. . . .

. . . .

Follow Madeleine's blog online at . . .
www.madeleinekaylive.com

For personal one-on-one coaching or consulting,
contact Madeleine at . . . www.madeleinekay.com

. . . .

Notes

Notes

Notes

Notes